How to Be Ha

The Ultimate Gui
Become a Happy and Confi-
dent Single, Starting Today

Harvey Segler

Free Bonus Content

Visit >>> ProjectSuperPerformance.com <<< to get free tips about healthy foods, meditation, productivity strategies and other nice tricks.

At the moment you can get a FREE download of :

"My 5 Favorite Foods For Higher Performance In Life!"

But hurry up, it will not be there forever!

Visit ProjectSuperPerformance.com And Download It Now! 100% Free! What Do You Have To Lose?

If you don't want the food tips, read the blog which can you who wants to be a super performer at work, as a parent, in school or maybe as an athlete.

Introduction

I want to thank you and congratulate you for downloading the book, *"How to be Happy Alone"*.

This book contains proven steps and strategies on how to find happiness even though you're single. It is a common misconception in the world we live in that we need to have a significant other in order to be happy.

Society tells us that we need to have that person to go to in the good times and the bad times, have that person to snuggle up with at night, and have that person to help with the bills and to be that person who is always blowing up your phone with cute little messages.

Or, if you are not having a significant other for the sake of your own satisfaction, society tells us to have one in order to prove to everyone that we can 'get' one. There is almost an unspoken mark of failure placed on singles, as though there is something wrong with them for not having a boyfriend or girlfriend.

Then, of course, comes the dreaded Valentine's Day. The stupid holiday that society has dreamt up that basically forces us to have significant others, otherwise risk enduring twenty-four hours of pity and single shaming by those who do have boyfriends or girlfriends.

This holiday has affected us so much that we have actually created apps to message us throughout the day and play the part of a significant other, just to look to the rest of the world as though we have one, or to make ourselves feel better about the fact that we do not.

That, my friend, is not how we were designed to be. Don't get me wrong, there is nothing wrong with having that other person, and there is nothing at all wrong with the cute messages, and the fun times you have together, or anything like that.

What I want to make clear is that while those things are all fun and good, they are not necessary for you to be happy. You do not need to have another person to be the happiest person on the planet, and there is no significant other that you can have that will make anyone think any more of you than they do right now.

You are all the validation that you need to be happy with yourself, and you are enough all on your own to show the rest of the world what you are made of. Just because you feel that you look better when you have someone hanging off your arm, you really don't.

"But I can't be alone," you say, or, "I don't want to die alone." A feeling that drives a lot of people to have relationship after relationship, even when they are not happy in them, or they don't like the person they are partnering with.

There is a truth, however, that may change how you feel about those statements, and that is the fact no one can make you feel any more or less alone than you are right now. At the end of the day, when you sleep, you are asleep alone, even if you are snuggled against someone.

While we are designed to want and like companionship, there are many ways we can get that without being in a relationship. It is a complete myth that you need someone else to be happy, true happiness comes from within.

In this book we are going to look at how you can become happy all on your own, whether you are currently in a relationship or not. You will see that it doesn't matter who you are, what you do for a living, or how much money you make, you will learn what it is like to be truly happy, and yet be entirely single.

Now, if you are currently in a relationship, I am not going to tell you to break up with your significant other, and if you are single, I am not going to tell you that you need to be opposed to a relationship.

What I am going to tell you is that you cannot possibly be happy in a relationship unless you are already happy on your own, and by going through this book you are going to learn how to be happy with you, just as you are, right now.

You will learn a new and amazing way of life. One that will enhance the relationship you are in if you have one, or a fact that will make you receptive to a relationship, but not make that be your goal.

You will find that you can be happier than you ever thought possible, and that it all comes from within. You won't have to spend a dime, or make any drastic change to your life, you are just going to learn simple little tips and tricks that will show you how to be happy, right here, and right now.

The only one who can make you happy, is you, and the only one who is standing in the way of that happiness is you. There is nothing on this planet that can touch that, and you are about to discover how to be happy alone.

What are you waiting for? There is a life out there that is waiting for you to live it. Don't waste another second waiting for that Mr. or Mrs. Right to come along, you are your own Right, and you have a life to live.

Thanks again for downloading this book, I hope you enjoy it!

Table of contents

Chapter 1: Love Yourself

Chapter 2: Healthy Lifestyle

Chapter 3: Find Your Passion

Chapter 4: Get Out of Your Comfort Zone

Chapter 5: Make Use of Your Alone Time

Chapter 6: Appreciate Your Life

Chapter 7: Being Pro in a Life of Cons

Chapter 8: The Ex Factor

Chapter 9: Approaching Relationships While Happy

Conclusion + Bonus

"Positive Thinking" Preview

♥ **Copyright 2014 by Anton Kimfors - All rights reserved.**

This document is geared towards providing exact and reliable information in regards to the topic and issue covered. The publication is sold with the idea that the publisher is not required to render accounting, officially permitted, or otherwise, qualified services. If advice is necessary, legal or professional, a practiced individual in the profession should be ordered.

- From a Declaration of Principles which was accepted and approved equally by a Committee of the American Bar Association and a Committee of Publishers and Associations.

In no way is it legal to reproduce, duplicate, or transmit any part of this document in either electronic means or in printed format. Recording of this publication is strictly prohibited and any storage of this document is not allowed unless with written permission from the publisher. All rights reserved.

The information provided herein is stated to be truthful and consistent, in that any liability, in terms of inattention or otherwise, by any usage or abuse of any policies, processes, or directions contained within is the solitary and utter responsibility of the recipient reader. Under no circumstances will any legal responsibility or blame be held against the publisher for any reparation, damages, or monetary loss due to the information herein, either directly or indirectly.

Respective authors own all copyrights not held by the publisher.

The information herein is offered for informational purposes solely, and is universal as so. The presentation of the information is without contract or any type of guarantee assurance.

The trademarks that are used are without any consent, and the publication of the trademark is without permission or backing by the trademark owner. All trademarks and brands within this book are for clarifying purposes only and are the owned by the owners themselves, not affiliated with this document.

Chapter 1: Love Yourself

Being single and alone seems difficult and lonesome. Many people think that a person's status contributes to his happiness. But while being single can be lonely sometimes, it doesn't mean that you'll always be happy otherwise. Whether you're single or in a relationship, you can feel both sadness and happiness.

Our brains are funny things, and so are our hearts. They always want whatever it is they don't have. For example, you may feel that you are unhappy alone, and that all you need to be happy is a significant other. So, you go out, you find that significant other, and you expect nothing but joy and happiness to be yours.

And it is. For a while.

Then, all of the other things creep in. The annoying habits that the other person does, the nagging of how they want you to change, the money for all of the things that they want to do. And it doesn't help that you see all those other people out there that seem to be happy, and attractive. You begin to tell yourself that you would be happy... with one of them.

So, you do one of two things, you either break up with the person you are with, but, believing you can't be alone, you jump right in to a new relationship, or, you wait it out in misery until your significant other breaks up with you, then you jump into something else, only to find that it is the same story with them.

Then the cycle begins again.

Repeating this cycle doesn't ever really bring happiness, in fact, quite the opposite. You see people reaching the point of saying "all men are pigs" or "all women are psychos" or "I'll just make the most of this because it's easier."

Essentially, they have just given up. They feel that there is no way for them to get along with the opposite sex, and have just resigned themselves to the fact they will never be happy. And, since they can't be alone, they feel that they need to just make the most of the situation to avoid the horror of solitude.

I am now going to take the opportunity to share with you a little secret. It is not the other person's fault that you are not happy. Nobody can make you happy or unhappy, that is up to you. Now, I am not saying that there are not people out there who are not good fits for each other, but what I am saying is that you should never seek happiness in or from a relationship.

Never put that pressure on another human being. They are not perfect, and they are going to let you down, every time. People make mistakes, and people can't be there for you any time of any day. Sure, you can be with someone who makes you happy, but don't expect them to be the source of your happiness.

When you learn that you can be happy alone, that is when you can be happy in a relationship. When you have a partner that enhances your life, then you will be happy. You don't need that person to make your life, you already have that, what you need is that person who makes your life better.

Now, let's take a look at how this all makes sense, and what you can do to make your life happy, all on your own.

Finding happiness while you're single takes practice, but if you really want to be happy, the first thing that you need to do is to start loving yourself. It may not seem easy, but if you will only follow the tips below, you will learn how to love your life even if you're not in a relationship with someone.

1. Happiness begins in you.

    Your happiness doesn't start from other people. No one can make you less happy but you. So, you have to stop relying on others to make you happy. A lot of people say that they are happy on their own, but they don't live like they are. If a person is truly happy with who they are and as they are, they don't need to have the validation from anyone.

2. Believe that you are awesome, just the way you are.

    Other people will feel if you're uncomfortable with yourself. Remember that you are unique and outstanding. You have something in you that others don't have, something that you can share with others to help the world become a better place to live. If you feel good about yourself, you will begin to see the world in a different perspective and you will feel happier about it. You will learn more about how you can feel better about yourself on chapter 2 and 3.

3. Respect yourself.

    Ignore the negative aspects of your life and focus on your positive aspects. If you want to be able to genuinely love yourself, you have to learn how to respect yourself. Keep in mind that you're human. Over time, you will commit mistakes and fall hard. You will find it hard to believe in your abilities and skills. But if you look at your wonderful side, you will value yourself highly and begin to respect the person that you have become.

4. Appreciate the person that you are.

   There's no better way to feel good from within than to appreciate your own personality. If you believe in yourself, you can do greater things. You won't be restricted by your limitations. Instead, you will find your limitations as challenges that you need to overcome. Appreciate the fact that after all that you went through, you were able to surpass all the problems in your life even if you're single.

5. Be highly motivated.

   Don't give up when the going gets tough. If you keep on pressing on, you will end up victorious. If you are able to achieve your dreams and overcome your struggles, you will become more successful in life. Motivate yourself to keep on living even if you have to push through life by yourself.

   Establish your own sort of rewards system. Don't be afraid to tell yourself that you are doing a good job, and that you are going to treat yourself as a result. Did you do well at work? Treat yourself to that new outfit or video game.

Did you reach a weight loss goal? Go get your hair done or by that next set of weights. There is nothing wrong with being the person who tells yourself that you did a good job. In fact, it is scientifically proven that we will work harder at something if we know we are going to be rewarded for it in the end.

6. Don't criticize yourself too much.

    It is sweet to be loved. Furthermore, it feels good to be admired and cared for. You feel happier when you love yourself. But these things take time. You can't have results overnight. So don't think lesser of yourself if you don't see changes any time soon. Allow the change to gently roll in and wait patiently for its effects in your life.

7. Do the things that make you feel beautiful.

    Whatever makes you feel beautiful, do it. Don't hold back from enjoying your beauty simply because you're single. Do something to make yourself feel beautiful from the inside.

8. Take care of yourself.

    Too often people who are not in a relationship tend to treat themselves one of two ways. Either they work out a lot, and do things they think will increase their chances at getting a boyfriend or girlfriend, or they take the opposite approach and do nothing because they figure since they don't have a significant other, then they have no reason to care.

I strongly encourage you to break out of this line of thinking, and to do the things that make you feel great. If you like to work out, do it for you, not so you can attract someone. Take care of your body and the way that you look for you and only you.

When you care about yourself and like yourself, it will show to the world around you, and you will feel a lot better about yourself regardless of your relationship status.

9. Take control, as a habit of life.

    If you are single, you will be in charge of your life entirely. Nobody can dictate your decisions; you choose things by yourself. This is a practice you need to get used to now, before you enter into another relationship.

    Too many people feel that singleness equals freedom, and relationships equal prison. This is not the case. You are a person who has your own mind, and you make your own decisions. You need to get used to that fact now, then make that quality something you look for in others.

When you are a person who can make a decision and stick to it, you will naturally stick with people who are the same way. This will make you a lot happier now, and in the future when you are in a relationship, you won't develop that co-dependency that ends up being so harmful to the couple.

People may try to suggest things for you, and that is something that will continue throughout your entire life, but you are the one who decides whether to apply those suggestions or not. So take control of your life and make wise decisions.

Above all, don't allow negativity to creep into your life. Accept that you can't be perfect, but don't stay in mediocrity. Always strive to be better, and have the attitude that you are on a journey. Work out to become the best of who you are until you learn to love yourself just the way you are.

Chapter 2: Healthy Lifestyle

Now that you've learned how to love yourself, it's time to keep yourself healthy and fit. Many single people ignore physical health because they no longer care about their life, or they try to get healthy thinking they will attract more people if they look better.

Both of those reasons are not good reasons to be healthy. You know that you need to love yourself, and you don't need to be appreciated by others in order to do that. Too often we get stuck in the rut of thinking that if we were just a little bit of this or a little more of that we would have relationships and everything would be solved. Unfortunately weight has nothing to do with the success of a relationship. But if you love yourself, you are aware that a healthy lifestyle can contribute to your happiness.

Staying healthy requires considerable work. You have to be mindful of your actions. You have to keep on doing things that could help you stay healthy. Moreover, you need to find different ways to avoid things that could risk your health.

Here are some health tips to help you get through each day:

1. Be mindful of what you eat.

   Single and lonely people fall into the habit of emotional eating resulting to binge eating. Stop eating too much. From now on, be mindful of what you allow to enter your body. Whatever comes in your body will generally affect your physical health. Start eating healthy food and feel good from within.

   If you don't know how to get a grip on this, try making a food journal. Record everything you eat, and how healthy it was for you. Keep track of portion sizes and how often you are eating.

   You may be surprised at how much mindless eating add up in a day, and how devastating the results can be on your weight and health.

2. Pack your own meals.

   Whether you're still a student or already a working professional, you need to bring your own meal to your school or office. This doesn't only save you time and money, but it also helps you keep your body weight on the watch. You will only feel the hassle during the first week of doing the routine. But once you get used to it, it will turn into a habit that you won't mind doing every day.

If you pack your own meals, you have the liberty to bring healthy meals instead of simply choosing from the varieties in the cafeteria. You are assured that your food is fresh and you don't have to worry about preservatives.

An added bonus is that you can always bring exactly what you like, and it makes for a good opportunity to discuss with other people recipes as well as weight watching regimes.

3. Try to crockpot your meals.

    Since you have to prepare your own meals, sometimes it's too much of a burden to go through the process of cooking. Either you don't have the time to stay in front of the stove and wait for your dinner to be cooked or you simply hate doing the task.

    By using a crockpot for cooking your meals, you can leave it right before you head to your office and you have your dinner ready for you by the time you arrive at home. Knowing dinner is already waiting for you when you get home is also a great motivator to cut down on afternoon snacks, or to swing by and grab some fast food when you are headed home from work.

4. Replace acidic beverages with shakes and smoothies.

   It takes less than a minute to blend your own smoothie or shake. In addition to being tasty and satisfying, smoothies and shakes are also the healthier replacement to your favorite soda and alcoholic drinks.

   Bear in mind, however, that smoothies can be loaded down with sugar. If you are switching to smoothies for health, don't get fooled into thinking all smoothies are healthy. Try making your own, and cut the sugar.

   Not only will they taste less sweet and more like the fruits they are made with, your waistline will thank you for cutting the calories that is in all that sugar!

5. Choose the right fitness program for you.

   Fitness programs don't have to be boring. There are many physical activities that are helpful and fun at the same time. Choose an exercise according to your taste. For example, instead of running every day, go swimming during the weekends. Both exercise can tone build and tone your muscles but swimming can be more fun.

Not into going out to workout? Not a problem! There are countless workout videos you can do right at home, or you can even look online to find some highly effective videos for free. This will give you the privacy of your own home, but you will still get all the results of one who spends hours in the gym.

6. Make fitness a priority in your life.

You may enjoy almost every kind of physical activity, but if you don't make fitness a priority in your life, you may easily put it off again and again. Make it one of the top priorities in your life by setting fitness schedules. Mark your calendar to make sure that you don't forget your exercise time.

It can be surprising to many people how little they need to workout in order to see results. You should make an effort to get your heart rate up for 20 minutes every to try a high intensity workout only every other day.

Write down on the calendar the days you workout, and see the results in the mirror in no time at all.

7. Pick your fitness goals wisely.

You can't be everything that the world tells you to be. When choosing your personal exercise activity, you might be tempted to choose activities that don't fit your profile.

The people in the magazines are not real people. They have been air brushed and photo shopped to look like they are flawless human beings, but they are just as real as you and me when they are walking down the street.

Don't ever pick a professional studio fitness picture as your goal of what you want to look like, and don't torture yourself to get there. Pick fitness goals that are real, and pick exercises you enjoy to reach them. Measure success on how you feel when you get up in the morning, and how you like yourself when you look in the mirror, not based on what the scale says.

Don't start running if the activity bores you. Don't play tennis if you have hand-eye coordination problems. To have a successful fitness program, you have to choose an activity that you don't only enjoy but you can also carry out regularly.

So there you have it, the tips that can help you stay healthy and fit. These tips will help you start living a healthy lifestyle, and directly put you on the road to loving yourself, and finding happiness outside a relationship.

There is a lot of joy found in reaching a goal that you set for yourself, and you will be amazed at how good you feel about yourself when you are capable of handling things all on your own.

If you think that you have a more serious health condition, don't hesitate to consult a physician. Do something about your health while you still can. Remember the famous adage: "Prevention is better than cure."

Chapter 3: Find Your Passion

Doing something that you are passionate about is one of the best things that you can ever enjoy in your life. Imagine living your life every day, doing the things that you love. You can never be happier than that. It simply is the best life to live!

This mindset spills into every aspect of life, whether you are trying to figure out what you want to do, or if you are just looking to be happy in your hobbies. A great rule to live by is to figure out what you love to do, then figure out how to get paid for doing it.

Not all of us can get paid for following our dreams or passions, but that doesn't mean that we can't all have passions that we do. Whether you make a living at it or not, you should be doing what you love to do, no matter what other people tell you.

No experience in your life is a waste of time if it adds to the person you are, and no achievement in your life is a mistake if it adds to the person you are becoming. We are all prewired to have passions, and if you are not pursuing yours, you will never be happy, regardless of being single or not.

Before you can find your passion, you need to know what passion is. Passion is not the same as hobby. Although you can do a passion for a hobby, these are not interchangeable terms. Hobby is something that you do to avoid boredom. It can be something that you enjoy doing or something that you are good at.

However, if you are passionate about doing something, you take time to explore it. You start with the basics but you aim for excellence. You enjoy doing it but you don't simply do it for fun; you do it because there's nothing you would rather do in your life. It doesn't matter if you are getting paid for it or not, and you don't care what other people are telling you about it. You know it is what makes you happy, so it is what you are going to do with your time.

Sometimes, though, there are people who don't know what their passion is. They know that there are things they like to do, but they don't know if they would call it a mere hobby, or an actual passion. Are you one of those people? Don't worry, here is a list of things you can do that will help you find what your passion is.

In order to find your passion, here are the steps that you've got to take:

1. Explore your interests.

One of the things that you love doing can turn into your passion. You may enjoy singing, writing, taking photos, cooking, or even creating something out of the ordinary, but there is that one thing that you are willing to do beyond mediocrity. You need to explore your interests in order to find out what it is.

2. Think about one thing that you want to do for the rest of your life.

After exploring your interests, determine which among those things do you want to do in your entire lifetime. It could be something that you have been dreaming of doing but you keep on putting off for later because you don't have time. Perhaps you think that it's too impractical or that you don't have the resources to do it.

It has been said that if you bother dreaming at all, then you should dream big. There is a lot of truth to this. The whole point of those day dreams that we pursue in our lives is to grow into that person we want to be.

If you keep your dreams at a small, and manageable level, you are never going to achieve that level you wish to achieve. Your life will just be stuck in the realm of being good enough, and that's about it.

3. Know your goals (and how to achieve them).

If you are passionate about something, you don't only do it whenever you have time—you make time to do it. Once you determined your passion, you have to set personal goals. What do you want to achieve in the future? For example, if you enjoy cooking, would you like to become a chef someday? If yes, where would you like to work? Are you going to apply at hotels or do you prefer to open your own restaurant?

Part of the reason dreams or passions seem to be out of reach is because you don't break them down into manageable bites that can be handled. You may love cooking and want to be a chef, but you are not going to walk into a five star restaurant off the streets and get the top chef position.

You need to start where you can, and build up. Find a restaurant that will hire you, get experience, and build up.

Make connections, move up the ladder, and talk to people. Yes, there will be times when the door is shut in your face, but don't let that discourage you, simply take a new direction and find a door that is open.

4. Set an action plan.

It is now time to turn your hobby into passion. Make a plan on how you are going to be better at your passion. For example, if you enjoy photography, enroll in photography class or join contests to expose your talent. Do anything and everything you can to excel at something that you are passionate about.

Take constructive criticism, and let the negative people roll off your back. Learn from the people that want to help you, and ignore the rest. This is your life and your dream, so let everyone that is holding you back go by the wayside, and listen to those that want to see you succeed.

5. Set a deadline.

Set a time frame so you will have a deadline to look forward to. Your deadline will keep you motivated in working harder to reach your goals. Don't give yourself permission to go past your deadline unless it is for reasons that are out of your control.

Sure, there are going to be times when you just don't feel like doing something, but when you let things go by the wayside once, it just becomes that much easier to let it happen again, and again. Some things that happen are out of your control, but don't start missing deadlines because you were taking too many lazy days.

If you don't think you can keep yourself accountable, find a trusted friend, preferably the same sex as you, and have them keep you accountable. When you are learning to be happy being single, you should always seek the company of those of your same gender.

Learn to break out of the need to have the approval and validation of those of the opposite sex. While there is nothing wrong with this, it will also keep you in the mindset that you are doing things to impress the opposite gender, which will, in turn, keep you in the mindset you need to find one to partner with.

Trying to find your passion may not be as easy as it seems to be. It may take some time, especially if you have so many interests in life. You may also find it difficult to find your passion if you are busy with your daily responsibilities.

If you're not getting any nearer to discovering your passion, here are some additional tips for you:

1. Take a day off from your personal and professional responsibilities. Refrain from doing anything to keep your mind free from distractions.

2. Go someplace where you can be alone. Avoid any contact from family, friends, and colleagues.

3. Take a few moments to relax. Free your mind from thinking about your unfinished tasks. Think about the present. Think about what you feel at the moment. When your mind is finally free from distracting thoughts, you will find it easier to think about the things that you love doing.

4. Keep a journal. You don't have to write a full entry in your diary. Simply take note of what happens in a day and write down anything that made you happy or anything that excited you.

5. Go somewhere you're never been before. Travel in strange lands and discover different values and cultures. Traveling experiences will fill your life with rich experiences that will help you find something that you love doing the most.

The road to finding your happiness is not easy. Nonetheless, don't give up so easily on your passion. As Ella Fitzgerald noted, "Just don't give up trying to do what you really want to do. Where there's love and inspiration, I don't think you can go wrong.

Chapter 4: Get Out of Your Comfort Zone

"To succeed, we must become comfortable with being uncomfortable on a daily basis," says Anthony Robbins.

Taking risks sounds challenging and scary. The technology has made life far easier now than it had been ten years ago, but that is not an assurance that life will never break or hurt you. Despite the high-tech lifestyle, you remain naive to life's roadblocks, heartbreaks, and challenges. Those things are enough reason to hold you back and keep you on your comfort zone.

While we all love our phones, tablets, and computers, let's face it. These things are not doing us any favors. We are more in touch with a screen than we are in the real world, and it seems that when we are forced to be a part of that world, most of us would rather lick concrete than say hello to someone face to face.

In your comfort zone, you are safe and sound. You can control your circumstances and you don't go beyond your boundaries. You keep your perimeter in check to make sure that you're not stepping beyond the world you're used to living. In your comfort zone, you can live a quiet, calm, and peaceful life. However, you will never experience the exhilarating feeling of overcoming your insecurities and flaws. If you are finally tired of living life the same way, it's time to go out of your comfort zone and start living the life of uncertainty.

Let's take a few moments to discuss the importance of going out of your comfort zone.

Everything that you do is a part of your comfort zone if it becomes a daily part of your life. It can be a part of your routines that you do without feeling uneasy or anxious. Often, people try to define "getting out of your comfort zone" as doing something out of the ordinary. But the truth is doing anything that makes you feel nervous and agitated is already considered as being outside your comfort zone.

This can be anything from going to a job interview, to meeting new people, to even talking on the phone. The thing about comfort zones is that no one person can tell another person what their comfort zone is. Comfort zones are as varied as the people who have them.

Generally speaking, anxiety is not a feeling that we enjoy but it can be beneficial for you. Studies show that when you do something that makes you feel uneasy, it will push you harder and make you work better.

In 1908, the study of mice proved that performance gets better as anxiety levels increased. However, anxiety can only help until a certain level – beyond a certain threshold, a difficult task combined with anxiety results to declined performance. The trick, therefore, is to step out of your comfort zone enough to get somewhere, but to do it in small enough steps that you can actually get there, and not just freeze in place.

Staying in your comfort zone can halt progress or improvement. This is an unlikely situation that you don't want to happen when you're single. Boredom usually strikes when someone stops from trying to do something extraordinary. In order to avoid that, you have to go out of your comfort zone from time to time, and discover more of yourself and give way for personal development.

Another thing that you need to keep in mind is you want to be happy single, and that is the key to being happy anywhere, but if you are not willing to step out of your comfort zone, you will never be able to meet that person and be in a truly healthy relationship.

Here are some tips to go out of your comfort zone:

1. Change your perspective in life. Think of something out of the box. Let your imagination flow.

2. Make yourself comfortable with uncomfortable things. Try to do small things that make you feel uneasy. For example, smile to a stranger while walking in the park. Do this for a while. When it becomes normal and natural, take it a step further, say hello. Keep moving onward and upward, and you will see results.

3. Challenge yourself. If you have a project that you think you can accomplish within a month, work harder and finish it in two weeks. Then, have the ambition to move on to another project.

4. Take one step at a time. You can't do everything overnight. Try to do one challenging task at a time and take time before you do another one. While you want to keep moving on, it is important to pause and reflect on your accomplishments.

5. Try to get comfortable, and see the humor when you make a fool out of yourself. You feel embarrassed when you say the wrong thing or you act the wrong

way, but that is just a part of being human. Everyone does it, and everyone expects it.

While you may be embarrassed that you did something in the morning, odds are the other people that were involved have already forgotten about it. Learn to lighten up and laugh at yourself. Do something silly every now and then, and try not to think of what others will think about you.

Like everything else discussed in this book, going out of your comfort zone is not easy. Don't worry if you think you're not making any progress. As long as you work on it, you are already improving. You will live a happier life when you don't stop doing things that challenge your emotional and physical comfort zones.

Chapter 5: Make Use of Your Alone Time

Many people say that staying single is a decision. But whatever the reason behind your single status, you have to enjoy the freedom of deciding for yourself. You don't have anyone to contradict your opinions; you can choose whatever you want to do or wherever you want to go. While you're still single, you have to make use of your time wisely and efficiently. You can stay up late doing what you want to, work hard, work out, play sports, take painting courses, whatever you want! It is your choice .But don't stay home watching TV, or of course, it is your choice but I don't recommend it. Do something valuable, something that you enjoy but also gives you some experience or some sort of reward.

1) First, you have to think about the advantages of being single. When you're in a relationship, there are so many restrictions and rules to follow. No matter how good the relationship is, you have limitations such as the way you spend your time and the people you can spend your time with. So for the freedom, be happy.

2) Create your own version of happiness. Read, dance, sing, or write. Just do something that you think will make you happy and spend more time in doing it. It's better than sitting in the dark corner of your

room and sulking because you don't have a boyfriend or girlfriend.

3) Enhance your talents. Enhance your skills. When you focus on becoming the best of who you are, you will feel a sense of complete happiness, satisfaction, and contentment that even being in a relationship cannot offer. You'll never feel as much accomplished as you would when you're doing the best in everything you do.

4) Do something that you've never done before. Run a mile. Stay overnight at a five star hotel. Go hiking. Just do anything that is interesting and fun.

5) Connect with people. Being in a relationship with someone requires time, and sometimes, it also means losing time for other important people in your life. So, enjoy the fun of being with your friends while you still have the freedom to do so. Yes, you can still do that when you're already in a relationship, but not anytime you want.

You have so much time on your hands when you are single. Make use of it and you'll feel better about yourself and your life.

Chapter 6: Appreciate Your Life

Don't feel bad about being single. No matter what your marital status is, people will find something wrong to talk about you. In the previous chapters, you were advised to accept the fact that you are human; you have weaknesses and flaws. If people truly care about you, they are willing to accept you, warts and all.

People tend to want what they don't have and can't appreciate what they already have. It's no surprise if you feel that being in a relationship is better than being single. Even though this is normal, you need to learn how to appreciate your life if you want to have a happy existence. Remember that happiness is not only found in being in a relationship. You can enjoy your life when you're single as much as when you are in a relationship. So how do you do it?

Here are some tips to help you appreciate your life:

1. Appreciate being alone. Even an introvert person finds comfort in the company of an extrovert. In this fast-paced society, you rarely find yourself alone even if you're single. But what you need to do is to learn how to love being by yourself. If you end up being alone on a Saturday night, find a way to have fun and do something that can make you happy.

2. Appreciate the fact that you don't have to share your space with someone. When you are living by yourself, you don't have to look out for someone else's mess in the house.

3. Appreciate that you don't have to deal with your partner's parents. Let's face it, some parents can be too controlling or manipulative. If you are in a relationship, whether you like it or not, you want to live up to the standards of your partner's parents. You don't want them to think that their son is dating a lousy girl. But if you're single, you don't have any expectations to meet. You can simply be yourself and no one would ask you to try to put your best foot forward on family reunions.

4. Appreciate the privilege to enjoy anyone's company without worrying about a jealous partner. You are free to talk and make friends with anyone you wish.

5. Appreciate the liberty to work on improving yourself. In chapter 5, you are told to make use of your time in honing your skills and talents. Being single is the best time to do so because nobody's around to nag you how to do things the right way.

Keep in mind that being single is the best time to fully enjoy your life and embrace every good opportunity that comes your way. So don't let it go to waste. Go ahead and celebrate your single-hood!

And in all of your enjoyment, take the time to figure out who you are and what you want in general. Maybe you don't want to enter into another relationship, or maybe you want to readjust your game and pursue dating in a whole new light.

People are attracted to those who know who they are, what they want, and how to get it. No one wants to get into a relationship where they feel like they have to then take care of the other person. Sure, it may seem heroic at first, but it is going to get old eventually.

This is the time in your life when you have the ability to try out the things you want to do, and you don't have to worry about how it will affect other people. When you realize what it is you want in your own life, you will be happy, whether or not you have another person to share it with or not.

Chapter 7: Being Pro in a Life of Cons

As we have mentioned in the last chapter, there are a lot of pros and cons to being single (or in a relationship). While it may seem like all the pros lie in being in a relationship when you are single, let me assure you that there are a lot of cons there, too.

For example, when you are dating, you have to take into account where the other person is, and what they are doing. It can be difficult to make plans, especially if you are living together. You may want to have friends over, they may have already invited their sister to come stay for the week, tying up the spare bedroom.

Then there is the money factor, what you spend your money on, how much of it goes to them and their activities, and what you can do with your own things now becomes a joint decision. There is so much more freedom when you are single, and you can find people who appreciate you and what you do for yourself.

You don't have to worry that the dishes get done every single day, or that the toilet seat is left up or down. Then there is the pet issue. You like cats (or don't) so get one, or you have the benefit of not having to put up with one. There aren't any birthdays to remember, or parents to meet, or anniversaries to have to worry about.

You don't have to go to that wedding for that estranged second cousin that you have never heard of, or worry that you are not making your partner happy. If you want to disappear across the country for the weekend, you don't have to check in with anyone, or wonder what they are doing in your absence.

Then, of course, there is the real kicker. If you are not dating, it is impossible to cheat on someone, or to be cheated on. There is so much less stress when you don't have to look at your phone and wonder why you haven't heard of them, or deal with that stomach ache because you are going to be out of town for a while and you hope they don't take advantage of that situation.

You can wear what you want, when you want, eat what you want, when you want, and make those crazy, life changing choices without having to worry they don't want to go with you.

Then, there are the smaller benefits that you don't even think about. You can stretch out and take over the entire bed, you can watch whatever you want to watch when you want to watch it, and there is no one there to finish the milk or the toilet paper and not tell you.

When you realize that you don't need to have the validation of a significant other, and that there is so much more freedom to not having one, you will begin to realize that you actually prefer the freedom that singleness offers. It is as though two chains melt off of you, and you can do what you want.

Sure, it does take some getting used to when it comes to the cute messages not being on your phone, but try to think back to the time when you didn't care if some random person missed you. If you have that desire to be 'missed' by something, get a pet, or think of your mother.

There are so many benefits to being single, you don't have to worry that you are not missed by someone 24/7, but rather that you have the freedom to do what you want when you get off of work, and since you didn't have to buy that expected thousand dollar Valentine's Day gift, you actually have the money to do what it was you wanted to do.

Chapter 8: The Ex Factor

It is no secret that a lot of people turn to books such as this one when they are hurting. If you are seeking to become happy while single, that implies that you are not happy now, and you are likely single.

The other truth is that people often feel least happy single when they are fresh out of a relationship, and this is the prime time when they are trying to figure out what they did wrong, and what they can do to bring their ex back.

Of course you want to be happy single, and that is why you came to this book to begin with, but many people feel that they are going to be happy, or try to be happy, single, in an effort to bring their ex back to them, as though some magic formula happens when you are single that will bring them running back to you.

I am going to encourage you to let all of those thoughts go. Your ex is an ex for a reason, and odds are you are better off without them. What happened, happened, and that is the end of that. You are going to be happy single, for the pure and simple fact it is what is best for you, not because you are going to win your ex back by doing it.

I am not trying to be insensitive or callous by saying it, and I freely admit that one of the hardest parts of being single is the beginning. When you have been in a relationship, or when you think that you have found the person you can picture the rest of your life with, it hurts when it doesn't work out.

There are all of those questions that come flooding in, wondering what went wrong, and what you could of done differently to keep them around, and why this, and why that, and the list goes on.

Maybe it ended on a bad note. Maybe there was cheating, or too much spending, or they didn't like this, that, or the other thing about you or your family, and that's way it ended. Maybe it was doomed from the beginning, and you only intended 'to have fun' but it ended in heartbreak.

Whatever it is, life on your own now feels like a monster of loneliness that just wants to swallow you up. It doesn't matter if you were together for months, years, or even just a few weeks. It also doesn't matter if they were your first, second, third, or fortieth heartbreak, it feels the same each time, and you have to recover and rebuild each time.

So what are you to do? Just pretend that it never happened? Label them as the evil person they must be for hurting you so much and never speak to them again? Or take that high and mighty route and try to remain friends?

Ultimately, that choice is up to you as long as it doesn't get in the way of your progress. Can you really be happy being friends with your ex, even when you see them with someone else? Are they the jealous type that is always keeping tabs on you and where you have been? Are you able to move forward, even keeping in contact with them?

If the answer is yes, you can be friends, and you can still move on with your life, then you are one of the rare few. Many people can't stay friends after a relationship, and there is nothing wrong with that. You need to do what is right for you to be happy, and if that means no contact with that person, no contact it is.

You have to avoid becoming stuck at all costs. No person on this planet is worth it, if they are causing a roadblock to you and your happiness. Sure, as we have said before, there is nothing other people can do to make you happy or not, but at the same time, you have to do your part.

If there is that person in your life, or who had been in your life, and they just can't be now for whatever the reason may be, cut them loose, cut them loose entirely, and cut them loose for good. There is none of that 'someday we can be friends' stuff, it does nothing for your progress, and it keeps you in the relationship mindset. You need to view life as happy on your own, and having that mentality that you need to keep that other person around isn't going to do anything to help you move on.

Everyone makes mistakes, you have to let it go and move on.

Another thing that will hold you back in your happiness, is to cling to what happened in past relationships. There were hurts on both sides, and things that shouldn't have happened but did. If you want to truly move on, you need to acknowledge that they did happen, and let it go.

While these things do hurt you, they are hurts that will fade if you let them. Don't be that person who has 'the story.' The one who walks around and is always telling everyone what happened to them, and what that person did to them. Relationships come and relationships go, don't be the one who is always trying to get the rest of the world to feel bad for you because so and so broke your heart.

Hold your head up high after a relationship, and be free to move on. Don't let them keep you stuck in what you were, and don't be defined by what happened. You know now what it takes to be happy with yourself, and that there isn't anyone but you that can make it happen, so let it go and move on.

You will find that all of those failed relationships will fade with time. Odds are you will always remember the people who were involved, but all of the details will fade if you don't dwell on them, and the thoughts of what may have happened differently won't matter anymore. What did happen happened, and you are a different person because of it.

So should you never get back with an ex?

There are a lot of different websites that are trying to tell you ways you can win your ex back, and have them come crawling back to you, but I encourage you to not worry about that.

In this book, you have learned that you don't need anyone else to be happy, and you are seeking to be happy on your own. If you are following the steps to being happy while single, you won't be worrying about your ex or how to get them back. If they are meant to come back they will, if not then don't worry about it.

You are going to be perfectly happy whether they do or don't, and you will find that the more you pursue your own happiness, the less important it will be to you that they come back. Sure, you may still think the world of them and wish them the best, but whether you date them again or not is something that doesn't even cross your mind anymore.

You will finally reach the level of letting those things happen if they do, but not worrying about it if they don't. Happiness comes from within, not from another person or a relationship status, so pursue your happiness based off of what we have learned in the earlier chapters, not whether or not you are going to impress others.

Chapter 9: Approaching Relationships While Happy

Once you are happy with yourself, you will find that you become a magnet to other people. Romantically or not, people are attracted to those that appreciate life, and appreciate those who are in it.

It's a common mistake that a lot of people make when they are in a relationship to only focus on the person they are with, and as a result they push away the other people who are in their lives. While they may not mean for this to happen, it does, and as a result they find themselves alone when they find themselves single once again.

Build strong relationships with everyone, and maintain them no matter what.

Now that you are single, and know how to be happy like you are, it is time to build relationships with people that will last even through your next relationship. You need to make sure that you don't ignore your friends, and make them a priority, even when you are in a relationship.

These are the people that are there for you through thick and thin, and if you feel that they wouldn't be there for you, you need to find friends that will be. Spend the time of being happy with yourself finding others that feel the same way, and who will build you up. Don't waste your time with game players.

True friendships are the ones that are built to last. And you will find that the happier you are with yourself, the more satisfying these kinds of relationships will be. You will be perfectly happy to talk to your friends about things, and go to parties with them, and not have to have someone else hanging off your arm to prove that you made it in life.

Everything will take on a whole new spin when you have real friends that will be there for you. Loneliness doesn't exist, and your self confidence will soar. It is almost as though you will have the emotional benefit of having a significant other, but you won't have the drawbacks.

Relax on the hunt, it will happen when it happens.

There is an earth shattering truth that helps a lot of people in their happiness while they are single, and I am going to share that with you now. While it won't solve any of your problems, it will help you with your stressing over finding 'the one'.

There is no 'the one' one.

Shocking, I know, but it's true. We as people are perfectly capable of being happy with a handful of different people. This means that there is no 'one' that you have to sift out in seven billion people, but rather you have to find someone who respects you for who you are, and supports you.

Someone who embellishes your happiness, and is happy with you. There are more people out there that are a match for you than you might think, and when you realize this fact, it will be a huge weight and amount of pressure off your shoulders. Stop hunting for that magical and elusive 'one', and live your life as you want to live it.

Sooner or later you are going to find someone who loves you, your passions, and has their own set of passions as well. You will find that they are a match to you not because you need them to complete you, but rather because you both know that you are happy as you are, and that you will be happy together.

Let your happiness keep you from settling.

Now that you know how to be happy, and that you don't need a relationship to be happy, you will be able to realize that you can have much higher standards than you had before in the relationship realm.

Now, you can find someone that you don't have to 'make it work' with, but rather, who is a compliment to who you are. As we talked about before, relationships can be constricting. You don't want that. Don't be with someone who has to know every detail about you or where you are at all times, be with someone who trusts you, and who you trust right back.

Take your time, live your life, and be ready for that person to come into it if they may. There is a definite difference between needing a relationship and being open to one if it happens. You want to be happy just as you are, and open to one if it happens, only then will you find you can be truly happy in any situation.

When you break out of the need to have someone else to make you happy, you will find that you are happy regardless of your relationship status, and therefore you aren't that worried about being in another relationship. This means that you meet people, you take people for who they are, and you are yourself.

You know that it may happen, it may not, but either way you are going to be happy, because you don't depend on others for that happiness. It is a really freeing way of life, and it isn't a lifestyle you are going to have to give up when you do meet a person you want to date.

Instead, you are a perfectly happy person either way, and someone who isn't afraid to live life to the fullest!

Conclusion

Thank you again for downloading this book!

I hope this book was able to help you to become a happy and confident single individual.

The next step is to put what you learned into action. Make use of the tips that you found in this book and apply them in your life. Today is the best day to make a difference in your life while you are still single. So go ahead and start living the life that you deserve!

There is the phrase that you are single and ready to mingle, but I encourage you to be ready to mingle as yourself. Don't throw yourself out there to have another cycle repeated, but truly embrace life for everything it has to offer, and let another relationship fall into place if it may, but never make that your goal.

You deserve to be happy, so what are you waiting for? Get out there and be happy!

Finally, if you enjoyed this book, then I'd like to ask you for a favor, would you be kind enough to leave a review for this book on Amazon? It'd be greatly appreciated!

Visit https://www.amazon.com/review/create-review?ie=UTF8&asin=B00XT7RPTA

To leave a review for this book on Amazon! Or just look in your order history.

And do not forget to visit

www.ProjectSuperPerformance.com To get your free downloads now. Yes! 100% Free.

For example you could download my eBook:

"33.5 Power Habits - Habits That Will Make You Happier And More Successful"

And don't forget to check my other book

"**Positive Thinking**: Go From Negative to Positive and Achieve Happiness, Increased Productivity and Success For Life"

There will be a preview on next page!

If you want to buy it visit http://www.amazon.com/Positive-Thinking-Happiness-Productivity-Negativity-ebook/dp/B014P7D654/

Thank you again and good luck!

Preview from "*Positive Thinking*"

I want to thank you and congratulate you for downloading the book, *Positive Thinking*.

This book contains proven steps and strategies on how to rid your life of all the negative thinking and destructive influences that do nothing but bring you down.

We all want to be happy in life, and as a general rule of thumb we do what we can to make our lives happy. We go to extremes to do things that will hopefully make us happy, whether it be buying things, going on exotic trips all over the world, dating, working, or whatever it may be, mankind is on a constant trek to gain happiness.

If you stop for a second and really give it some thought, you will see that I am right. Everything we do and say is for the hopeful end result that we will then be happy with our lives.

Maybe if we made more money we would be happy. Or maybe if we had more friends, maybe if you looked like that person or lost 5 pounds, then you would be happy.

I hate to be the one to say it, but ultimately those things have nothing to do with how happy you are. That is why you see people who are simply stunning to look at, have more money than they know what to do with, and all the comforts that you long for, yet they are still not happy.

What makes this seem even bleaker is the fact that there is no magic formula for happiness, you can't ever make the right number of anything to ensure you will be happy tomorrow. The newness wears off of any new relationship, things get old and break.

Even after a long vacation you have to deal with the stress of going back to work, figure out what you missed, what you need to do now, and how you are going to pay for everything you did when you were out and about in the world. And after all of this dies down, you start to feel overwhelmed about your life once again, then it isn't long before you are hoping to go on another vacation.

But this can't be it. There are a lot of happy people out there. Chances are, you know a few of them. They are those people that just go about life, and no matter what their situation is, they seem to be happy.

There doesn't seem to be a thing on this planet that is able to shake them. They are clearly the 'glass is always half-full' types, and it doesn't seem to matter if it is hot, cold, windy, rainy, sunny, or anything.

In fact, they may be dressed well, dressed poorly, rich, poor, struggling... who knows? Yet they always seem to be happy. It is almost as if you can't bring them down even if you tried.

Of course there are the other people in the world, too. Those that have everything handed to them, and have the most cushioned life that someone could ask for, yet nothing is ever good enough. They manage to find fault in everything, even if it is something they thought they wanted.

These people are everywhere, but they don't seem to have the same power as the positive thinkers. Those that are positive just seem to rise above the crowd and do their own thing, and not let themselves be bothered by what is going on with the rest of the world.

So what is their secret? How did they manage to reach this level of happiness, and is there a way you can get it for yourself? Do you have to be some sort of superhero to feel happy that often, or is there really something simple that you can learn to do that will help you to also be that happy?

Don't worry, these people are not superheroes, they have just figured out what it means to think positively. Positive thinking is powerful, and it changes how you view every aspect of your life.

No matter what you may be going through, there is always a reason to be happy, and thinking positively will help you achieve that.

By the time you reach the end of this book, you will be able to:

- Think positively no matter what your situation is
- Find the good in everything
- Look up, and not down, when bad things happen
- And learn to apply this thinking to every aspect of your life

No matter who you are or what you have been through, you will be able to also learn the art of positive thinking, and in no time at all you will notice a drastic... and positive... difference start to take root in your own life.

So what are you waiting for? There is a life of positive out there, just waiting for you to join in.

Thanks again for downloading this book, I hope you enjoy it!

If you want to read more, get the book on: http://www.amazon.com/Positive-Thinking-Happiness-Productivity-Negativity-ebook/dp/B014P7D654/

And again, thank you for reading "How To Be Happy: Alone" Please leave a review by visiting:

https://www.amazon.com/review/create-review?ie=UTF8&asin=B00XT7RPTA

Thank You!